Hyacinth
12/30/2013

Unveiling the Enigma of
INDEPENDENT SCHOOLS

<u>From</u> the Perspective
of a Veteran Educator

Dr. Hyacinth C. Foster

INKWATER
PRESS

PORTLAND • OREGON
INKWATERPRESS.COM

Scan this QR Code to learn more about this title

Publisher: Inkwater Press | www.inkwaterpress.com

ISBN-13 978-1-62901-030-4 | ISBN-10 1-62901-030-8

Printed in the U.S.A.
All paper is acid free and meets all ANSI standards for archival quality paper.

1 3 5 7 9 10 8 6 4 2

Table of Contents

Acknowledgement

The contents of this book represent my perceptions of three independent schools. My views are based only on my observations and experiences. There might be many other stories to be told from the various perspectives of my fellow educators. However, I am anticipating that this book provided the much needed insight into the independent school environment by exposing the creative spirit within an environment that allows young minds to flourish. In contrast, there might be demoralizing consequences, not only on students, but on all members of the community when leaders are not held accountable.

The completion of this book was realized with the encouragement and support of my children and my sister, Madge George.

To Nwanyidimma Nwanneka Chukwujiorah and Camille McCaul-Matlack (my children and former students)… It is complete!

To all my former colleagues, thanks for your

willingness to allow me to learn from you and I hope you did learn from me. You know just why I had to write this book! I want to thank Kayla Farnan and Lisa Knight who listened to and offered useful suggestions as I wrote each section.

To Nicole King, Marsha Jones, and Joe Appiah who provided positive and tangible support to ensure that the book would become a reality.

Prelude

My entire teaching career in the United States encompassed a journey in independent school teaching. Prior to my arrival in the United States, I was engaged in public school education on the island of Jamaica, in the Northern Caribbean. It was by accident that I became a teacher in that system, but I learned much about the process and nuances of teaching, in particular the importance of collaboration among teachers, students, administrators, and parents. In addition, I learned that the profession, if taken seriously, would become a passion, and not just a job!

There was no conscious effort on my part to become a science teacher. However, I was always interested in science. During my second year at the University of the West Indies, there was a shortage of science teachers in many high schools on the island of Jamaica. Officials from the Department of Education visited the campus and asked those of us who had been given Government scholarships to help during the crisis, ON A TEMPORARY BASIS. One other condition was that if potential teachers gave five years of service to the government, we would **NOT** have to repay student loans. I volunteered and this would be my introduction into educating others. I had hoped to continue my studies as a medical doctor but faith had different plans. My temporary life as a probationary teacher began at an all-boys school, Kingston College, in the capital of the island.

However, in Jamaica, a prospective teacher could only teach for one year at the high school level. At the end of that time, the potential teacher had to receive the necessary teacher-education training to continue in the teaching profession. Maybe, I would not need that training because I received quick and surprising induction to the process of teaching in the first few days of my sojourn at the all boys' school (Adapted from Lessons from the Heart: Navigating Life). Well, the offer was too good to refuse! I could not believe that if I taught for five years, I would not have to repay the student loans—an exciting and sensible offer—Why not take it? I did, and that was the beginning of my educational learning and teaching career. Not to worry, I was learning so much, and teaching at an all-boys school was presenting a new set of challenges that I thoroughly enjoy, therefore I continued and received the teacher training I needed.

The training process offered by the University of

the West Indies was vigorous, exacting, intense, but innovative, and would serve me well when I migrated to the United States. In addition to learning how to teach and engage in educational research, I had a mentor (a University Professor) who stayed with me during my first year of teaching. I was able to ask questions, design science curriculum, express my concerns, and receive answers that helped me to grow as a teacher. However, once I became a resident of my new home (USA), I was encouraged by many to never enter the public school environment of Brooklyn, New York. I did not listen! I was determined to use the skills I had developed, put those ideas into practice, and prove my newfound theory. The theory was that—the focus of the educational process should be on the CHILDREN; that PARENTS were not the enemies of the process, that TEACHERS were the force that could change the way children viewed the world, and ADMINISTRATORS were the supporters of the children, the parents, and the teachers.

To begin my adventure, my first task was to investigate how to become a certified science teacher in the public school system of New York. I spent many hours completing the New York State's teacher application forms, requested my transcripts from the University of the West Indies that had to be sent from the institution to the certification office in Albany, and WAITED. In those days, there was no way of submitting information through the

Internet or by fax. So, as you may well imagine, it took some time, but eventually I was informed that I needed to sit an examination as part of the New York State's certification process.

No problem! I was prepared! Until, I found that I had to take three New York City trains (The *L* to the *A* to the *J*) to make it to the examination site by 7:30 a.m. on a SATURDAY morning! The final train, the *J* train did not seem to have a specific schedule on a weekday much less on a weekend. In the mid-1980's New York, the *J* train was known for its frequent mechanical stoppages that could happen at any time and at any point on the journey. Anyhow, with a 5:30 a.m. departure from home, I made it to Lower Manhattan just in time for the start of the examination. Well that was the easy part!

The examination began with uncharacteristic punctuality at 7:30 a.m., with General Knowledge. That portion of the examination included tests in literature and fine arts, followed by mathematics, followed by science, and followed by social studies. Surprise, there was a 10-minutes break! Just enough time and good luck that the line for the ladies' room would move fast enough to allow all of us to enter! Once we resumed, it was time for the listening, reading, writing (multiple choice), and writing (essay portion) of the examination. Would lunch ever arrive? It did, and lasted for **all of 20 minutes**! However, this was a Saturday and the nearest **bodega** was 15 minutes away. With no feasible option, many of us satisfied our hunger with a drink of water, and tried not to listen to the incessant rumbling of our stomachs, for the next hours of testing! Well, you can imagine that my thoughts were, "I only need to become a certified, science teacher and be able to TEACH! With that intermission, Part 1 of the test had ended!

Following the lunch break, it was on the afternoon session, where I completed the professional knowledge section of the examination. That portion consisted of six different areas that would be used to evaluate the knowledge that I possessed that might make me a competent teacher. The areas included—student development and learning; instruction and assessment; the professional environment, and finally, the instruction and assessment segment that was a constructed response assignment. The examination ended at 5:00 p.m. and by that time, not only was I exhausted physically, but also I was mentally depleted, and if asked, maybe I might not even remember my name! This was my introduction to bureaucracy and officialdom of one system of our government, and **Oh, what an induction!**

The Process...

My initiation into the inner workings of our educational system of government was just beginning! I would have to wait several weeks to learn whether I would be able to apply for provisional teacher certification. Then, I would have to visit the main education office where I would learn about potential teaching positions. Then, I would need to apply to principals of those schools; hope to get an interview, and finally a teaching position! Since the wheels of the process were moving so slowly, I could not afford to wait because the start of the new school year was just weeks away.

As I would learn, the provisional teacher certification was good for only five years. If one did not acquire a Master's degree in Education within the five years, then one would be eliminated from the profession. *I am hoping that by now, the year 2013, that there exists a speedier system of response for this process!* Often, I wonder if there are any similarities, and what are the differences, within the teacher-certification process within other states? Does the variety of certification processes impact the way teachers teach and children learn within our culture? Years later, I would learn of a different system of teacher certification when I relocated to the city in the southeastern United States and began the application for certification.

However, let me stay on task with my teacher-certification PROCESS! Since there was uncertainty regarding **when** I would receive notice of success or failure in the examination, I investigated and found out for the first time, that there was another world of education in the United States of America—<u>**INDE-PENDENT SCHOOLS**</u>! There were a few private schools in Jamaica but nothing compared to the world that I was about to enter! I researched the process for securing employment in the system, found an Independent School Agency, applied for a job, went to an interview, and was ready to begin teaching on September 1, 1985. A side note, it would be near the end of the the first semester before I received a letter stating that I had passed the **New York State's Certification Test and that I could proceed to find a teaching position!!!** However, I received the cautionary note (**in bold**) that the **provisional** teaching license was *only valid for five years* if I did not complete the master's program in education.

Indepedent School #1

My journey into this independent school environment began with an introductory lesson in *progressive* education. The principles and ethos of that *pedagogical movement* would continue to influence educational philosophy to the present day. The philosophy of *Independent School #1* was based on educators using the technique that might enable students to develop their own identities, while finding ways to incorporate the community into the learning process, since we are all social beings. Although, the original educational emphasis was on the visual and performing arts, other areas would gain equal status in promoting the development of the whole child. I would eventually develop an affinity for the principles of progressive learning. Those values were based on learning through doing, and my interest was heightened since the concept of experiential learning was related to the **SCIENTIFIC METHOD**—the basis of my science education.

Synopsis of Progressive Education

Based on my understanding and additional research, I came to recognize that although John Dewey and other educational researchers received credit for the progressive educational approach; there was actually no single source for the instructional concept. The aim of progressive education was to find ways to change the traditional approach to learning and teaching. I was on a new cultural and educational learning curve! The premises of the progressive approach might be perceived to be at the opposite end of the spectrum of the teaching process in Jamaican schools where the ideas of instruction and learning were imbibed in the British colonial educational system.

Continued Journey

In this independent school, I was on a revolutionary journey of learning. The more I learned, the more I became attracted to the approach of learning and teaching. I discovered the principles of individualized instruction, although much of the instruction was conducted through small-group interactions (mainly 8-12 students). This was a strange occurrence for me because, in Jamaica, I had grown accustomed to teaching thirty-five students during one class period. In addition, the independent school provided a variety of resources and encouraged me to develop skills in science teaching techniques to meet the needs of **EACH** student in any group. Although there was a specific text for each group, the emphasis was always on research and project development. Since then I have come to recognize any textbook as just another source of information that children might use to supplement the learning process. But, I have heard in passing, that the textbook ensures that parents understand how well their tuition payments were being used.

As the years went by, I developed the perception that I was a truly competent teacher, I knew my biological concepts, was skilled in teaching them at any level, but there was so much more to teaching as I would continue to discover. At *Independent School #1*, I would learn that the focus on the democratic process of learning and teaching would ensure that students became active participants in the learning process. Under those principles, students developed understanding and became involved in the political, social, and economic decisions of their world so that they could become participating citizens.

To achieve that stage of development, students embraced a healthy respect for diversity, became critical thinkers, and increased social intelligence. Teachers became active participants, in the process, by buying into the idea of classrooms where all could share ideas, use any and all approaches to help students learn, incorporate experiential learning opportunities into the curriculum, and understand that students and teachers were partners in the teaching and learning process. Later, as I became an educational researcher, I would come to understand more about the process and John Dewey.

During my sojourn at this independent school, I had to adjust to idiosyncrasies that I considered unheard of during my teaching career in Jamaica. The school focused on developing individual relationships with students and so I learned about the importance and function of the term **advisor** and **advisory**. First, each teacher participated in learning the required techniques, took on the role of advisor, and was assigned seven or eight students. Most times, the students were from one grade level, however, teachers could be asked to be in charge of an advisory that consisted of students from two grade levels.

In time, the advisors became the social and academic connectors, for all students, between administrators, other teachers, and parents. The school established a specific time during the weekly schedule for advisor/advisee meetings. The activities during those sessions were varied and ran the gauntlet from social activities designed by students to analysis of students' academic progress. Depending on the grade levels of the advisees, the role of the advisory might emphasize social skill development (9th grade), social and service skill opportunities (10th grade), or focus on college and career readiness (11th and 12th grades). Students in lower grades always looked forward to moving to the upper grades to experience the novel activities of those advisory sessions.

Furthermore, those advisory programs supported the school's programs, the student's progress, and parent involvement. During my continued educational journey, I discovered the benefits of allowing students to engage in the *small picture* to develop social integrations before meeting and extending participation in the *big picture* social interactions. Years later, I would recognize how the technique of *small picture* learning would be a successful technique that allowed students to understand *overarching* principles of scientific knowledge.

Independent School #1 was unique in so many ways! It would be well into my first year that I would learn that the school did not consider admission tests as a requirement for entry to school. Instead, students had to engage in carefully crafted interviews with the administrator and two teachers. Then, I had to learn that I would no longer be called Mrs. Foster instead I would be called **Hyacinth**. Adoption and adaptation took on new meaning! Again, a major departure from my teaching experience in Jamaica! Well, if I thought that was major, No, there was more to come... There were no number or letter grades and no formal structure for getting students to pass exams for entry to colleges! So, my first thought was did I set myself up because I just could not understand how this would or could work!!

My Learning and Teaching

Time is certainly the master of any of life's learning process. At *Independent School #1*, I was assigned to the Middle School (a new term for me—Grades five through eight). As I began my new assignment of teaching this age group, for the first time in my career, I met the most knowledgeable, intelligent, and caring leader, Evelyn M. She guided my learning as I was given latitude to design curricular materials appropriate for the age group. With a well-stocked science laboratory, the limits of teaching and learning were unending. My greatest accomplishment was in skill development on integrating

students' personal experiences into the science cur-riculum. The approach was so unlike my teaching and learning in Jamaica where I had followed a care-fully, crafted syllabus. **Often, I wonder if such leaders are lost to the profession.**

Further, this was the first time that I really understood the importance of students giving back to society. This independent school was truly part of the wider community. On a daily basis, various individuals and parents were always dropping in on classes; many of those individuals lent their exper-tise to support the teaching process. The influence of those individuals extended beyond the class-rooms, and as educators, parents, and students, we went on trips to museums, theaters, and the mon-umental sites in the city. We cleaned up the parks, planted vegetable gardens on the roof of the school, and visited and served at shelters.

Those were just the perks of my new journey in teaching. The second bonus came when I had the privilege to work with an outstanding group of educators who had such high self-esteem, confidence, and knowledge that teaching became sheer joy. Those individuals included Ray G. and Susan M. (Social Studies), and Ann S. (Art). The administration and the teachers were never threatened by the knowledge that others possessed. That fact gave us all a real opportunity to allow students to become totally involved in learning science, the arts, and every subject in the curriculum. I found creative ways to teach the science principles, students became excited, and administrators commended teachers for well-done jobs. The actions of all teachers were causes for yet one more celebration.

Memories are made of These...

Our weekly staff meetings were the greatest journey in learning to collaborate and learning to teach. In those staff meetings, educators and administrators shared ideas and found ways to communicate those ideas across the curriculum. We found time to visit each other's classrooms, and no one became intimidated by a visit from a colleague or any administrator! Those meetings were unlike future experiences in other staff meetings that were conducted by those in charge with limited opportunities for in-put or teamwork.

Those staff meetings were memories that would stay with me when I had to attend future meetings that did not measure up in content or procedure. At *Independent School #1*, teachers were treated to catered food and drink during the staff meetings. During those Wednesday meetings, the administration made sure that there was surplus so that we did not have to go home and cook for our families. We got specially marked dinners for each person's family. Those simple acts pointed to the considerations that were afforded all staff members by the institution.

In addition to being part of a caring community in small and large ways, I also internalized major teaching philosophies from this institution about the way a good educational institution functioned and should function:

1. **THE ADMINISTRATION TRUSTED THAT TEACHERS WOULD DO THEIR JOBS** (so there was no need to micro-manage the educators).

2. **EVERYONE WAS EXPECTED TO BE HONEST UNDER ALL CIRCUM-STANCES.**

3. **WE WERE IN THE *BUSINESS* OF**

ALLOWING EACH STUDENT TO REALIZE HIS OR HER FULL POTENTIAL.

4. OUR STUDENTS WERE THE FIRST PRIORITY.

5. MISTAKES WERE THE TOOLS THAT WE LEARNED FROM—ACKNOWL-EDGE MISTAKES, FIX THEM, AND MOVE ON.

6. DO NOT BLAME OTHERS...THE BLAME GAME LEADS TO DISCORD.

7. IF THERE WAS AN ISSUE WITH ANYONE, SPEAK WITH THE INDI-VIDUAL FIRST.

8. COLLABORATION WAS THE KEY TO LEARNING! YOU DID NOT HAVE ALL THE ANSWERS.

9. FIND YOUR VOICE AND USE IT.

10. PARENTS WERE NOT THE ENEMIES OF EDUCATORS.

Those were the principles of true education! Those suggestions and ideas made you just get up and want to go to work every day. My room on the fourth floor was a haven and comfort away from home.

It did not matter that I had to begin each day's journey with the *Dollar Cab!* **Yes, in 1985, it cost only one dollar for the ride from my home on East 56th Street, in Brooklyn, New York to Flatbush/ Junction!** I would then take the Number 2 train from the Flatbush Station (last/ first stop on the line however, you see it) to West 59th Street in Manhattan. No, that was not the end of the journey! If all went as planned that leg of the journey would take about 1 hour. Then, I would have to wait for the Number 1 train! I could only hope that train would come on time, and if it did, I would spend another 10 minutes on the train. Finally, I would exit seven blocks further up the Hudson to *my new home away from home!*

There were days when my mother instinct would over-rule my educator's instinct. At those times, the fear would surface as to what to do if one of the children became ill. I had to regain my composure since there was no need to worry at this institution! The leaders of *Independent School #1* expected you to take care of your child or children and they would do the rest. Furthermore, another area of potential stress was pro-actively resolved. In the 80s, the trains were not always reliable, and so in case of lateness, all teachers would leave information for the first lesson of the next day prepared and in a place that was accessible. *The welfare of the students was of utmost importance*!

Collaboration—It Matters!

Parent involvement was an integral part of the learning process. Parents were never classified as *helicopter parents,* as I would hear expressed, for the first time, at another institution. To this day, that term continues to irk me. I would later perceive that many educators who engaged in the negative view of parents were those who lacked confidence in their knowledge and skills as instructors. At *Independent School #1*, the input from parents was welcomed and appreciated and many volunteered to bring their professional skills to the classrooms. Students and teachers enjoyed visits from artists, doctors, nurses, caterers, and writers among others. I am not sure how each child felt when the parent arrived to participate, but those visits were a source of excitement and elevation for the learning process.

Adjustments and Adoptions

As I continued on this teaching and learning journey, I had to adjust to the absence of students in uniforms. In Jamaica, the students' uniforms easily identified each school. The schools where I attended or worked had unique colors such as **cream blouses and skirts with green ties and belts; or khaki pants and shirts with purple and white ties; or burgundy tunics and white blouses.** Those color combinations would become important when schools competed at the regional and national sports championships. So, where were the uniforms at my new school? There were none! The dress code was simply—**BE APPROPRIATELY DRESSED.** And, I learned quite quickly that the word **APPROPRIATELY** meant different things to different people and especially to teenagers! Among the clothes worn by the students, there would be no rhyme and no reason to the styles and colors! Some skirts were short, **VERY SHORT**... others were long... **VERY LONG.** Many times the colors seemed to be combined as if in competition with each other, and not many pieces were ever graced by an iron. In addition, I did observe that the condition of some apparel deteriorated as the semester progressed. Unless the outfit reached to the level of *OUTRAGEOUS*, administrators and teachers did not reprimand students, because they were learning! **The institution had its priorities in a straight line!**

The students at *Independent School #1* did not wear shoes and socks that matched carefully starched and ironed uniforms, as was done by my former Jamaican students. Instead, students wore sneakers that were mainly white however; they could at times be pink, yellow, or any color in between. Clothes and shoes were not the only unique features. The females would include colors in their hair, and those colors seemed to change with the seasons. Some would start with orange as the year began in September, in celebration of fall; changed to orange or pink as spring approached, and finally dirty-blond to match the gold graduation gown that would be on display in June. That observation has remained with me since I traversed the evolution with my daughter!

Several other adjustments would mark my sojourn at that institution. Whereas, I was used to weekly meetings for worship at the schools in Jamaica, I was introduced to *assemblies*. There were no prayers for guidance during the week instead; we were entertained by the dramatic skills, the dancing skills, the artistic skills, or the science, math, and technology skills of our students. Yes, that was the time of an adventure into the intricacies of emerging technology! **THE YEAR WAS 1985** and you, have to remember that as a country, (USA) we were just on the threshold of **COMPUTERS AND TECH-NOLOGY** invasion. As educators, we never had an inkling, but we were about to learn much more about ways of integrating teaching and technology into so many academic subjects. Yet, there was still **ONE** constant in that STRANGE NEW WORLD—**SCIENCE FAIRS**—that followed me from my teaching in Jamaica! As I reflected during this writing process, I can certainly find meaning in the statement: *Oh, how times have changed but they remain the same!*

Before the Advent of Computers!

Remember, as I pointed out before we had very few computers for students or teachers in 1985. A science fair production was a labor of another nature! Science teachers began by introducing the concepts that would evolve into topics. That process was followed with each student developing a unique outline based on the scientific method procedure. Students went to the library (opened for extended periods during those times) to begin research on individual topics. Soon, the typewriters would be in full production mode. If typewriters were not available, then students would begin using *NOTE CARDS*! As a side note, there were no colorful note cards, just **WHITE**! Once the science research was completed, students would begin the process of presenting their work on the tri-fold presentation board (**the same as we have today... THAT HAS NOT CHANGED!**) Since many students did not have computers and printers, stencils and colorful construction paper became the student's best friend.

Many hours were spent decorating those boards with *title, background, hypotheses, materials, procedure, results, conclusion, and bibliography* in the most skillfully stenciled operation. That was when educators and students learned about true collaboration! Students who were great artists would help others to design their boards. Those who had great writing skills would assist others with getting the information on the display boards. Others would search magazines for appropriate pictures to apply to the boards.

As the process continued, other teachers (those who were not science teachers) would help to edit the information, mainly for spelling errors. Remember, we did not have the computers so there was no spell or grammar check available. That progression had to be completed for every student before the work was pasted first on construction paper, then on the display boards. As educators, we did learn how to deal with stress or emerging frustrations!

The rechecking process had to be done if projects were to be entered into the City's Science Fair. The City's competition would usually be a two-day event starting on a Friday morning and culminating on Saturday evening with the awards presentations. Again, helping the students to gain external recognition was a community event. The group of helpers included the science teachers, administrators, teachers of other subject areas, and parents. Yes, I was tired after the event; however, those were exciting and rewarding times. Satisfaction came from seeing the look of joy and achievement on the faces of the students, parents, and the administrators. Remember, *Independent School #1* was not considered an institution that focused on the sciences. However, those and similar events would begin the change in the school academic reputation within the community. During my years at the school, science became one of the highlights of the instructional practice. Eventually, we developed new curricular material so that qualified science teachers taught the science concepts from Kindergarten through 12th grade. The transformation in the sciences spread its tentacles to all other areas of student learning!

Experiential Learning

Our community outreach trips took us to famous places in the City! As we learned in the classrooms, our learning took us on visits to many sites including the *Museum of Natural History, Bronx Zoo, Brooklyn, Manhattan,* and *Washington (BMW) bridges, Brooklyn Botanic Gardens, Cathedral of Saint John the*

Divine, *Central Park* (our outdoor science classroom). In addition, we traveled to *The Cloisters*, *Ellis Island*, *Empire State Building*, *Madison Square Garden*, saw the entire City on the *Circle Line*, and enjoyed the taste of the ethnic cuisines as we visited numerous restaurants. Teachers and students developed a great appreciation for the process of teaching and learning as we all recognized that what we were doing in our school was reflected in our daily lives.

There was low attrition of students and teachers at *Independent School #1*. Departures occurred when teachers retired or moved on for personal reasons. The majority of students left at the end of 12th grade, however, on occasion others left for other personal reasons. It was always gratifying to see that the number of students increased during those years. As a staff member, there was no fear or threat of being relieved of your duties. This was a safe community of administrators, teachers, students, and parents.

Social Interactions

That was the professional side of the process but there was a social side. As educators, we celebrated all that was there to be celebrated—birthdays, new births, awards for achievements in every area of student life, teacher accomplishments, football, baseball, basketball and track, every holiday, art shows, language successes, and end of the year festivities.

For the staff, we developed a tradition of celebrating each other. At those celebrations, each of us made ethnic dishes that we shared. So, we enjoyed *Frites,* Chicken Sausage Gumbo (French); Pescado Frito, *Patatas Bravas* (Fried Potatoes in Spicy Sauce courtesy of Spain); taco recipes, Acupulco chicken (Mexico); New England clam chowder, peach cobbler, and pizza (America); shepherd's pie, roast duck, and fish with chips (British); and curried chicken, oxtail, rice and peas (courtesy of Jamaica). The venue for those gathering differed each time we met. Some day we would be on a 14th floor apartment overlooking the Hudson River; the penthouse of an apartment on the Upper West Side of Manhattan; or an apartment in downtown Brooklyn.

Well, as I adjusted to the life in my new institution, I continued to acclimatize to the culture of the United States. My Jamaican accent did not change, but gradually, as students learned more about the location and culture of Jamaica, they began to experiment with the accent, they listened to Bob Marley's song, requested recipes, and came back to tell others about their visits to the island. This was now GLOBAL education. However, as the saying goes—all good things will come to an end!

Change: Nothing Stays the Same

The first change came at the end of my third year

when the Head left, and Mr. C. became the new leader. He continued to promote the philosophy of progressive education so there were no VISIBLE internal changes. All things went on as usual with the social and professional life of the school. However, the atmosphere within the institution was not the same, and there was an emerging feeling of apprehension! That emotion would come to reality in the next school year.

In 1988, the entire community was called to a meeting. Present at the meeting were members of the entire school board, administrators, teachers, staff, and parents. At that fateful meeting, we were informed that the school was facing financial difficulties and would be forced to declare bankruptcy. The reason given was decline in enrollment, elevated cost of maintenance, and fall-off in gift giving. Still, the leaders assured us that we still had our jobs. All employees were asked to continue performing tasks as before, and the leaders would do whatever was necessary to keep the school afloat. *AFLOAT!! NOT A GREAT WORD TO DESCRIBE ANY SITUATION!!*

The school year, 1989, came and we still had our jobs, the students came, parents were visible, and the school was once again buzzing with life. However, it was difficult to live with the daily question of WHAT WOULD HAPPEN? The school year progressed and in December, ANOTHER MEETING

WAS CALLED... THIS SURELY WAS IT!... **But, it was not!** At one meeting, all members of the community were told that the Board had come up with a solution that would involve **MERGING OF INDE-PENDENT SCHOOL #1** with another school. This term became part of my vocabulary long before the word (MERGE) would become a daily occurrence among major organizations in the United States.

So, what would **MERGING** mean for our jobs! Well, nothing in the immediate future. It would happen in the next school year (1990)! At the start of that school year, the high school students began temporary classes at the other school's building. However, my science classes continued uninterrupted at *Independent School #1*. The change had arrived and all prior feeling of happiness evaporated from the once calm and inviting environment. This was just the prelude because in February 1991, the leaders called the community to yet another meeting! This time, we were told that with the approved merger some staff members would not be invited to continue. In addition, the head of Independent School #1 would be leaving. *Luckily or unluckily, the new administration invited me to stay.*

Expect the Unexpected

The first step in the *staying* process involved a meeting the new head of school. Well, I went into the meeting with all good intentions and expectations. However, little did I know, I would not leave that meeting on a high note! As we came to the final stages of the meeting, and I was about the sign the contract for the next school year, the following exchange occurred.

Headmaster: Oh by the way, I see that you are an *ALIEN*!

Me: Excuse me, Sir. This is the first time that I have been described using that term! Are you suggesting that my home is on *MARS, NEPTUNE, or JUPITER!*

Headmaster: OH, NO. NOT AT ALL! NOT AT ALL!

ME: So would you please explain your prior statement?

Headmaster: You have a *GREEN CARD*?

ME: YES. And?? Before he could interject into the conversation, I continued...

ME: Well then, I believe that would make me a stranger to this planet from *URANUS* (Blue-green planet). And, I continued...

ME: I think we need to end this conversation and I will not be able to accept a position with your school! However, I am confident that I will read about you and the school in the future! Thank you and have a great day.

With that, I asked to be excused and left his office. **_I WAS UNEMPLOYED, AGAIN!_** Then and there, I began my application to become a citizen of the United States of America. No one would ever speak to me in such a condescending manner again! My former administrators and colleagues wrote a letter about the situation to the Board and there was much anger expressed, but I was on my way out. I completed the school year on a high note while seeking employment elsewhere. I had forgotten about my statement until in 2003, I did read about the headmaster. He did make the headlines when he was arrested (for reasons I would not discuss), and would never be in any school system again.

Accepting Change and Moving Forward

A new chapter was about to begin in my life as an educator, if I did find a JOB! Once again, I considered the public school. However, I had just a year left on the Provisional Teaching certificate, and I was not sure that I could complete the required degree in that time. In addition, my daughter was a student at _Independent School #1_, and I had to find an appropriate school for her. This was yet another example of the lessons that I have lived with—one's actions always come with consequences! Well, I would accept the consequences and move on! Unlike my prior experience with finding a job, at this point, I did not feel so alone or scared with the pending job search because I had a network whose members were also in search of work. Once again, I contacted my trusted Independent School Employment agency, and as if on cue, I had my first interview at the end of March, 1991. I was no longer naïve! I did not expect to find discrimination so alive in the independent school community. **The experience opened my eyes and made me so aware of the overt and subtle forms of inequality that existed.**

Indepedent School #2

There were to be many positives around my entry to this educational institution. First, the commute was about 1/3 the former journey. Second, one of my former colleagues would be interviewing for a position at this new school, and third, I met the headmaster, James H. who exuded kindness, peace,

intelligence, and a love of people, especially children during my initial interview. And yes, he did not ask if I was an *ALIEN*!

I continue to marvel about that interview because the session lasted way beyond the allotted 45 minutes. At that point, the interview became a discussion of ways to revive a science program, revive a high school that was teetering on closure, and my continued professional development. The conversion was riveting that I almost forget to find out if my daughter would be able to join the community in the coming school year. However, I did not have to worry because before I could ask, I was offered a Middle School teaching position on the spot, and Trudy would become a new member of the school's 9th grade.

The new opportunity filled me with excitement, and even though I had not met any of my colleagues or the students, I knew that I had found **MY NEW HOME**. That institution would indeed be my home for the next 15 years and years after I left! My job began on September 1st, 1991. I was to begin my journey as co-advisor of the 5th grade and I was destined to meet another great Head of Middle School Head, Dianne Mc... She was knowledgeable about students in this age group, she was a confident administrator, and so she gave the staff the full range to develop and create curricular materials.

As I began the new venture, I would continue

to recognize that a teacher's assignment was closely connected to the student enrollment of the independent school. As a result, in later years, my teaching assignment would always change depending on the number of students in the institutions. In my first year, as I said before, I was a co-advisor to 5th grade students; a middle school science teacher of 5th grade and 7th grade; and a 9th grade general biology teacher. The assignment required daily movement from one floor to another since the middle and high schools were in separate areas of the school. As with the movement to different areas of the building, I became skilled in how to balance conversations, as well as science content, and skills between middle and high school students. In addition, I had to develop a separation line between my role as a teacher and parent, within the same environment.

By the end of the first semester, I began to feel exhaustion from the constant brain and body stimulations. I really did not know if I could survive; much less continue to the end of the year. Although I did not do much complaining, the headmaster who visited every classroom, each Monday morning, was so supportive that I found the courage to continue. I wanted the high school to survive and succeed so I vowed that I would continue at all cost. In addition, I knew I did not have the energy to go on interviews again, nor could I move daughter again since she had adjusted so well to the new environment.

As I reflect on my teaching journey, I have yet to meet another Headmaster who knew and cared so much about each teacher, the teacher's family members, and the teacher's development. Each Monday morning, he arrived as if on cue and kept up a lively, short conversation that made one feel needed and special. **Maybe schools could benefit from this unique approach of leadership**!

Unique Culture Does Make a Difference

Independent School #2 was unique in other ways. The philosophy of the institution was grounded in Quaker principles! Members of the community did not have to be practicing Quakers, but the beliefs were so engaging that one found oneself internalizing the ideas. Since my first year at that institution, I have maintained my focus on the tolerance and acceptance of others, promoting and celebrating cultural, ethnic/racial, gender, and learning differences, as well as being content in whatever state I found myself. Those were the easier tasks, the more unique ones were yet to come, and I had to get accustomed to the distinctive terms such as *Collection*, *Meeting for Worship*, and *Consensus* that were foreign to me as to the new students. I can recall with a smile on my face the number of students who asked me how much money they should take to *Collection*! I did explain as I was learning that *Collection* was similar to *Assembly* in other schools.

It was not so easy to explain *Meeting for Worship!* During those sessions each week, the community met, in groups according to divisions, or on special occasions as an entire school. During the initial staff meetings, administration explained the terms, but I would come to understand that there was truth in the idea that <u>to do is to understand</u>! Based on that lesson, I have continued to allow <u>students to do so they understand</u>.

Since my first *Meeting for Worship,* I have never had a more exceptional, amazing, or unique experience, and I doubt I will have another similar encounter. Let me explain, as a group we walked down to the school's Meeting House or if the event was special we travel a longer distance to the Quaker Meeting House. Students would always be talking with each other on either journey! However, as we approached the venue, the chatter would decrease. As we entered and took our seats, the entire group would fall into complete silence! It was unimaginable and the silence was frightening! It would be several months of this repeat activity before I lost the intimidating feeling.

Still, there was more to learn about this process! Before the start of the *meeting*, we were asked to **CENTER** our thoughts! That meant clearing our minds of all concerns! Easier said than done!

To move the process along, there were times, when a query was sent to the group in advance of the *Meeting for Worship*, and we were asked to express our thoughts on the topic. Please understand that this was not a **DISCUSSION** session. You stood up, stated your opinion, and you sat down! Others were not allowed to comment on your ideas! **YOUR IDEAS WERE STATEMENTS THAT STOOD ALONE!** That entire scenario was occurring as the silence continued. Each speaker had to sit down, before another individual could stand up to speak.

At other times, individuals spoke as their *INNER SPIRIT* led them! You might just imagine the range of thoughts that such an event would present! We would hear about people's observations as they traveled on the subway; information about someone's experience at a marriage, funeral, or other event; some social injustice; a place where the school community could offer some assistance; or someone giving thanks to another individual... and the range of topics went on and on! So, how would the session end? Well, one of the leaders would stand without making any comment, and that would be the signal for the end of the *Meeting*! As the years went by, I would learn and assimilate the ideas around the *INNER LIGHT* that each individual possessed, how to speak from that *LIGHT*, and how to become surrounded by the *LIGHT*!

During my years, at *Independent School #2*,

students frequently let out a groan when they had to fulfill this weekly requirement of ***Meeting for Worship...*** Statement such as: Not again! I'm tired of it! I need to go to the Nurse's Office!... were common complaints. However, as I continue to talk with alumni, many credited the *SILENCE* as one of the best activities that has remained useful in their lives. Years later, as I reflected on the positive aspects of the process, I realize that the activity was an exceptional way of helping students to respect the opinions of others while developing public speaking gifts.

From the **<u>Silence</u>**, we might hear an opinion about social injustice, the experiences with the commute, or a joyful or sorrowful announcement. I grew to recognize the importance of empathy, and I believe that all my students did understand the importance of being selfless as we as a people focus on others.

As an educator, I found that the use of silence before each class and at the end was a sound practice that allowed students to express what they hoped to achieve from each class, and close with the new ideas they had gathered at the end. I continued to put that idea into action even after I left *Independent School #2*. **Maybe, educators could incorporate this action in their daily work so students will understand their importance in the learning and teaching process.**

Good so far! However, I still had to learn the meaning and function of ***consensus***. Actually, the process involved _consensus of opinions_ but many people consider the term excessive, so that they simply say _consensus._ This was a technique used to arrive at agreement on any topic. It would be many years, before I could fully grasp the concept. During many discussions, the educators could find similar ground and so the ideas moved on to the next level of implementation. However, in some meetings, the ideas were not easily accepted. Therefore, we went with the opinion(s) of the majority.

Philosophy—How Much Love Enters the Process?

Independent School #2 did not ascribe to any one educational philosophy, but rather as educators, we claimed the idea that each child had an **_INNER LIGHT_**, was unique, and **_COULD LEARN_**. Therefore, it was our duty as educators to help each child discover this **_LIGHT_** and learn. And, we did! In every class, the students' abilities ran the spectrum and so as educators, we became adept in cultivating and developing the unique qualities of the students. As the years passed, I discovered that with encouragement, guidance, trust, and **genuine care**, students do develop a love for learning. Although, the former _Independent School #1_ had a philosophy that was steeped in progressive principles, this school embraced those ideas and travel much further along the spectrum of positive ways to educate children.

Schools can say a lot about their beliefs and philosophies but it is only when an educator enters that true beliefs are exposed.

So, what do I believe are the reasons for revival of the high school and survival of *Independent School #2?* Those reasons embrace the gauntlet of all who entered the doors.

1. *The headmaster was skilled in both education and business principles, he believed in each member of the staff; he promoted useful professional development of the staff.*

2. *The headmaster knew and was genuinely interested in the welfare of each child, and parent or guardian.*

3. *The headmaster had a visible presence throughout the school; and above all, he maintained a true open-door policy where each person was expected to say exactly what was on his/her mind without fear of retribution.*

4. *The headmaster ensured that financial resources were located to provide all the equipment and materials needed to ensure success of the learning process.*

The administration provided the science department with a budget and teachers were allowed to request the materials that were needed to teach

each class. All materials and equipment were purchased during the summer before the start of the new school year. Further, teachers received *petty cash* for purchase of perishables and they just had to provide the receipts for such purchases at the end of each month! The staff appreciated the burden of not using personal finances to make incidental purchases. Even an act such as this provided for a stress-free environment for the teaching staff!

Other Distinctive Happenings

As my learning continued, I would come to understand that there were graduations and then **THERE WERE GRADUATIONS!** *Independent School #2* engaged in a **CELEBRATION for GRADUATION**. The festivities began with an Awards Ceremony that lasted many hours. It felt as if every student received one award or another. Lest you forget, we started with our **PERIOD OF SILENCE!!** The next day, we would meet again in the early afternoon, for the **GRADUATION MEETING FOR WORSHIP!** This could go on as long as necessary. One hour, or two hours was not unheard of! Once again, we sat in silence and anyone could begin the *Meeting*! There was no limit to what parents, students, family, friends, and staff would say as they expressed pride in the graduates. One year, the meeting went on for three hours so the school had to find a way to revise the process! After the first year when the *Meeting for Worship* and Graduation were combined and resulted in a four-hour marathon event, through consensus we separated both activities! In time, we would meet for the period of silence directly before the graduation ceremony.

Following the Graduation's Meeting for Worship, we celebrated with a **GRADUATION DINNER** that was previewed by the senior Internship presentations. During such an event, we were always treated to meals from all over the world based on the nationality of the student population. The function would begin early evening and last way into the night. The next day we would be ready for the Graduation Ceremony. Students would have the practice session of how to enter, collect diploma, and exit!

The **GRADUATION CEREMONY** was unusual to say the least. Students did not wear gowns so you can imagine that the podium would represent the colors of the world with dresses from "mini" to ankle length; males would wear *regular* outfits! Gradually, the staff and students decided that there needed to be some normalcy to the dressing while allowing for individuality! Even those modifications that eliminated **TIGHT** shorts were arrived at through CONCENSUS! In the early years, we started in the Meeting House then eventually we graduated to more sophisticated environment. The event was simple and unique, one or two speakers, a slide show showing students progression from birth to the present day; a statement from each graduate; handing out of diplomas and snack afterwards. With that, the graduates were on the journey to capture new worlds!

Growth and Development

It was fun to be at this school. The administrative team was knowledgeable and confident in the ability to perform their duties. Together with the headmaster, they employed individuals who were intelligent, creative, self-assured, and loved educating children. As a result, when those groups came together, there was minimal animosity since all arrived with a high level of self-esteem, and the focus was always on educating the child.

The teachers, at all level were creative, and innovation reigned within the school. As educators, we were allowed to develop curricular material that would bring out the excitement and was in line with all the advances in every subject areas. While *Independent School #2* was surround by many other independent schools that espoused excellence in student learning; the enrolment of the institution continued to increase from 50 students in 1991. During those years, I developed skills in being a teacher, an advisor, an assistant dean, head of science department, a

board member, and a member of a strategic team for school improvement.

During my years of teaching and administrative experiences, I successfully mentored and supervised staff members, coordinated the needs of the science labs, facilitated the needs of promising students (via internships), coordinated science fairs, developed grant-proposals and maintained my active role in continued professional development. In one year, we received so much grant money, that we were able to outfit the entire Upper school with *MAGNAVOX Desktops*!!!

In addition, I was also the teacher of 9th grade general biology, 11/12th grades advanced and advanced placement biology, and Pre-Engineering elective to juniors and seniors. My children, Trudy and Gregg, would eventually attend and graduate from that institution.

With the new vision for creating a model science program, all of educators put creative skills in high gear! The most important was that we all had prior experience so we were able to incorporate our curricular material to meet the needs of the various age groups. In addition, as we built the curriculum, we had to keep in mind that if students had to leave the school, their knowledge and skills would allow for easy transition.

Building a Unified Curriculum

Once we (the teachers) developed, the core science subjects—Biology, Chemistry, and Physics—we began to focus on extension and enrichment programs. As a result, the advanced courses in the core subjects were phased in each year. Then, we went further to introduce Ecology, Environmental Science, Architecture and Pre-Engineering, and Robotics. In addition, we developed and linked the computer studies with the robotics curriculum, but the integration of technology into the other core subjects would become a gradual process. Finally, for those students who wanted to sharpen their skills in science even if they would not go on to study science at the tertiary level, we introduced Introduction to Chemistry and Physical Science.

By the third year, our efforts and the newly designed robotics curriculum were given much acclaim so we received funding to develop a robotics curriculum for middle school students. Students were becoming less fearful of the science contents because they could feel the excitement of the staff members who were so knowledgeable. Instead of just meeting the three-year science requirements for graduation, students were doing a fourth year of science studies. Many students began applying to do tertiary studies in the sciences. By the fifth year, we had students studying architecture, medicine, engineering, and computer sciences at the tertiary levels.

Our program extended beyond the classrooms. We ensured that students received additional stimulation as they visited the *Museum of Natural History, the Science Museum in Queens, Dolan DNA Labs, the Science Museum of New Jersey, and the Computer Museum of New York*. We walked the Brooklyn Bridge and learned its history and allowed our thoughts to center on those who gave their lives to build the structure. We also used our knowledge of that bridge to build our scaled models in the bridge building courses. We took journeys on the *Circle Line* as we investigated and created replica of the New York Skyline.

We walked the *Millstone trail* as we traveled to Dead Horse Bay. Even with all the changes in New York City, it was an environment where only minimal transformation had occurred. In that place, we found remains of our past as a City. The beach was littered with the vestiges of horses that were replaced when the automobiles took their place; soles of shoes, pieces of metals, and rusting telephones from the 1800s. However, *Dead Horse Bay* was the perfect environment to observe the ecological concept of *succession,* where as trash washes out to the ocean, new species were colonizing the beaches.

Our institution was socially aware. We visited the South Seaport to understand how the foods we ate entered the city. We journeyed to restaurants to learn about the diverse cultures of the City. Coney Island beach became our playground and learning ground as we investigated ecological concepts. We cleaned and painted parks on our service days. We worked in shelters and fed those who had no permanent home; we built furniture and cleaned the rooms at the Quaker Home for AIDS patients. Each new day brought new adventures and new learning.

Successful Change

In the sixth year, we developed a month-long internship for graduating seniors who would come back to share their experiences just prior to graduation. By that time, we were repeat performers in the yearly science fairs within our school and the New York City Science Fairs. The summers saw many students taking on internships in their area of interest. That was truly an exciting place to be a learner and an instructor.

Independent School #2 crafted my path to learning and teaching and I made lasting friendships at that institution. Room 401 was my haven and was always occupied by students. In addition, there were crises that on reflection were sources of wonderful memories:

1. The day a student decided to pull on the emergency shower just to see how it worked

and flooded the entire area from the fourth floor to the lobby.

2. The day a member of the science department decided to investigate the workings of a laser—BAD IDEA! He almost shocked himself to death.

3. The day a student although being warned not to place any metal objects in the electrical outlets, did so anyway, and sat for several minutes with electricity traveling through the body.

4. The day a student who was told not to eat in the lab, did so anyway, and had to be taken to the hospital where the stomach was pumped.

5. The day of our department's holiday party when one staff member decided that to just stand in the middle of Atlantic Avenue instead of crossing—we did convince the individual that that was not a good idea!

6. Being lost in my OWN neighborhood after the party at the Russian Restaurant that lasted longer than anyone anticipated.

Life at this institution was not always without some negative incidents, but they were resolved with tact and finesse. Even if we disagreed on professional ideas and levels, this was a family! We enjoyed each other's company and so we socialized. The science department was known to have Friday evening socials. This was not exclusive and anyone who wanted to attend was welcomed. As a group, we had beginning and ending staff parties. For a time, they would take place at one staff member's home, but often other staff members would volunteer their homes. The social events would last way into the night and the conversations were always uplifting— **WE WERE FAMILY!** Even as the enrollment grew, the same events continued. Changes were a part of our lives and sometimes they were never easy to work through or accept. However, everyone would soon learn that the modifications would benefit us all in the **future**.

I refuse to look on the any negative during those years, and that is how they will remain. The year before I left *Independent School #2*, I was selected as Teacher of the Year and was celebrated by the students whom I had taught for fifteen years. Below are some of my favorite students who have impacted my life as an educator at *Independent School # 2*. Each one made teaching a joy and I know they will go on to conquer the world.

Those students taught me the meaning of patience, kindness, how to deal with adversity, laughter, humility, and above all honesty. During my years, I became the mother to many! Each day after school ended, students who just wanted to learn filled the room, because they wanted to learn. School ended at 3:00 p.m., but as Trudy and Gregg grew older, I would find myself spending late hours and weekends getting my students ready for in-house and external science fairs. *My students simply wanted to learn and that was the joy of teaching!*

The students and parents in this *Independent School #2* were grateful to teachers and they showed their appreciation in many ways. Those are the simple acts that allowed educators to know that they are indeed making an impact on the next generation. The following excerpts developed that understanding for me, and my students may recognize some of these statements. Those sentiments set this school apart from other INDEPENDENT SCHOOLS!

Thankful Spirits Showing Appreciation

I have been in your class for 3 years in high school. But I never felt like only a student. You have always been there for me to help me and ensure that my broken foot did heal. You have been like my second mother. You always encouraged me to do my best. I know you cared about the students and show that inside and outside the school. I will always remember you as an angel because that's what my Mom calls you.

Thank you for taking care of me like a son and helping me though it was not mandatory to do so. God bless you. He has given you a heart of gold and I only wish the best for you in the future. I will never forget what you have done for me since 9th grade.

You are definitely an angel sent to help and guide our souls. And I thank you for everything you have done for me. You have helped me stay strong, positive, and healthy. You will always have a place in my heart.

I'm graduating from Brown because 4 years ago, you did everything in your power to pick up the pieces after my mother left. I'm going to UPENN law school and school of social work next year. I will be pursuing my Masters in Social Work and a law degree. I owe my education to you, and fully recognize that your helpful efforts extended well beyond the responsibilities of a teacher.

I can't begin to thank you for all you have done for me. I know that without you in my life, there is no way that I could have made it this far. Your role in helping me, guiding me, teaching me, and caring for me has gone above and beyond that of any teacher I can imagine. The love I have for you is so great, with honor and respect. I am proud to call you my teacher and to have been your student. As I move on in life, I can only hope that somewhere down the road God will bless me with another mentor as caring and giving as you. There is no way that I or anyone in my house can forget you. The world is lucky to have someone like you to be a part of it.

††

We were truly blessed for having M. to stay with us. I know that M. was blessed for having to spend an entire year at your school. Thank you for your kind and outstanding work with M!

††

I thought Mother's day was the best time for me to show some appreciation because you're one of the ladies that make sure I do right. You may not know this but the love I have for you is very great and insurmountable) hope I spelled that word correctlyJ) Thank you for all that you have done for me within the past four years, and I will really miss you nest year no matter what school I attend. I also really want to thank you for making me understand who I am as a person, and for being my support during the times when I found myself in trouble!

†‡

There are not enough words to explain how grateful I am to have you in my life. I appreciate all the things that you have done for me. I'll never forget you. Remember that you will always be like a mom to me. I am going to miss seeing your face.

†‡

I'm sorry I didn't get to see you at the end of the year. I wanted to thank you for all that you have done for L.. It's easy to see why the kids love you so much.

†‡

My child did learn so much from you, and as his parent, I learned so much too. There are no words in the English language to tell how grateful I am for all that you have done for L..I am eternally grateful, and would always remember, all of your kindness.

†‡

Thanks for 4 years of love and care. You will always

have a place in my heart. Do not worry; I will make you proud in college. Of course, you know I will still have to call you.

†♀

I've adopted you as Ma # #. You've done so much for me. I can't even begin to say THANK YOU enough. You've inspired me to succeed. I'll do just that and more. You will ALWAYS have a special place in my heart, now and forever.

†♀

On Saturday mornings, I do this tutoring thing with high school students. I tutor them in both **Biology** and English. The Biology part is great because I am learning along with them sometimes (but I have to act like I know what I am doing to impress the kids—ha! Ha! Anyway, we dissected a pig a couple of weeks ago, and it was amazing. I saw the heart, lings, spleen and everything else... and when I touched them ...wow! I've never felt like that before. To actually see and touch those things... I know you know what I am talking about; you have done it so many times before!

†♀

How can we ever begin to say thank you for all you

have given to our family. You have been there for J. and B.—taught them so beautifully, appreciated and loved them, always been caring and honest with the. This has been so clear to us and so very appreciated—What more could you ask for your children? You have also done this for us parents. How lucky we have been to share your generosity, love, and wisdom. We will never forget!

†‡

Thanks for all of the talks and dedication you have shown and given me. I'll never forget you and I'll always love you. You have been like my 2nd mom. Thank you is not enough words to say all my feelings. The only thing left for me to say is I LOVE YOU.

†‡

I would like to thank you for all the time and help you have given me. I really appreciate it! You are a very beautiful and generous person and that is why you are one of my favorite people. You are like a second mother to me as well as a lot of people. I'm really going to miss you and I will never forget you!

†‡

Thank you so very much for supporting me this year and helping us all through a tough time in our lives—Thank you for all the laughs and hugs when I most needed them!

†††

I had only one class with you but since then you have not only been a special friend, but a second mother. You were there when I needed your help, and you were there to straighten me out when I needed to be. I am really glad you were there for me when I needed somebody to talk to! Thank you for all your help in my senior year. My family and I would not have been able to do it without you. I have so much to say and I don't know how to say it. I will just thank you for being you!

†††

In an African village, an individual's accomplishment is the accomplishment of the community. Thank you for your support, love, friendship, undying commitment to the Upper School; but most of all, and your prayers.

†††

At first you scared me a lot, but now you still scare me but in a nicer way! You have helped me to excel in my chosen profession, Biology, as well as given me faith when there was no more left. You expected a lot from us and that's why I expect a lot from myself. Although it has been rough towards the end of the year, you have never thought twice to say a kind word in my direction. I didn't believe that many of the colleges I applied to would accept me because I needed so much money and my SAT scores were low, but you made me apply anyway! I know you believed that I would be accepted to all of them! You must get a lot of these cards, but I hope mine is especially special!

✝✝

Thank you for everything. Thank you for your words—the happy ones and the powerful ones! I will never forget you. I know that you love having flowers in your room, so I hope you like your vase. And the lotion is for all kids that come in and out!

✝✝

I have had an absolutely wonderful time at this school. I hope the traditions will never be discarded... Anyhow, whatever happens, I realize that I was lucky enough to have you as a teacher, a teacher who really embodied the philosophy at the school through her teaching, and by being a friend of all of the students. This has been a very stressful year for me. However, you have always been able to cheer me up and encourage me whether it be by simply smiling at me, telling me am hilarious story, or giving me the perfect words of advice. Thank you so much!

I must share one indelible experience that made me understand the importance of FAMILY in a workplace. *Independent School #2* had become one of sharing and caring. I wish that atmosphere would return to our institutions of learning. As the years passed, students were returning to speak about their experiences and share their motivations with the younger students. Those unexpected visits allowed us to know that we were doing a great job of educating the next generation. However, changes do happen and while we could understand and accept the internal changes; the external catastrophes are not always easy to deal with and do impact an individual for years to come.

One <u>Awful Experience of My Life</u> was dealt **with in a unique, caring, and professional manner**! Tuesday, September 11, 2001 began as any other day but would end in a most unusual way. Although I was not in any of the impacted areas, I realize that the cataclysm would affect my students, my colleagues, and me for years. I will share the impact on me as an educator, and my students as well as how this Independent school used its pro-active stance rather than a reactive attitude to help us all through the indescribable situation. **I ENCOURAGE OTHER SCHOOLS TO LEARN FROM THOSE ACTIONS!**

That Tuesday morning, I did not have a first period class, so I worked at setting up my lab equipment and materials for the class that would arrive at 8:50 a.m. Several students arrived a few minutes early, attendance was taken, and students began to review the laboratory procedures by 8:55 a.m. when suddenly, the fire drill bell broke the quiet! I knew the precise time, 8:56 a. m., because I looked at the clock. As members of the staff, we were always informed of the times of the fire drills before each was conducted. You may wonder why. Well, the kindergarten students had their classes on the 7th floor, and as a requirement of our service to each other; the seniors were asked to go upstairs to accompany those younger students to the lower gym.

So, an unannounced fire drill took us by surprise, but we quickly got in line to move from the 4th floor to the lower gym. We were about to leave when one of the administrators came around, almost out of breath, and told us to remain in our room, and sit on the floor. This had never happened before, that last request only came in the face of major thunderstorms (NOT USUAL IN THE CITY) or some catastrophe! As a community, were now accomplished in being **SILENT** and without a word, all students became silent. However, the tension in the room was almost visible. Without any further instructions for about 10 minutes, I recognized that fear was taking a visible toll on the faces of the students.

We were in that position until 9:05 a. m. and at that moment; I perceived that we were engulfed in a disaster, something we had never experienced before! A short time later, another administrator came with the news that not one, but two planes, had flown into the North Tower of the World Trade Center. My room # 401 had a clear view across the Brooklyn Bridge with the Towers in the distance! I was transfixed because at that moment, although the information was about two planes in the North Tower, I could not see what was happening at the South Tower, I could only see a bright yellow glow!

That vision has remained with me ever since! As I stood transfixed, the yellow glow was suddenly mixed with papers, white dust, and dark masses falling at the same time! Later I would learn that the dark masses were actually my fellow human beings free-falling to the ground! At 9:30 a. m., the administrators asked us to proceed to the lower gym, and when we got to our destination, students, administrators, faculty, and staff was informed of the emerging events.

What was so special about the way the institution handled the devastation? First, we were together as a family! The administrators and staff remained calm even though we were trembling in our shoes. In the silence, the news spread that all entrances and exits of the city were closed; the airports were closed; the subway screeched to a halt! So, how would parents get to their children? More was to be added when we were told that we would not be able to leave until the last child was picked up! We became resigned to do our duty to the children and ourselves! NOTHING MORE COULD HAPPEN! IT WOULD BE OVER SOON!

That was not the case as the news became more morbid by the hour! By this time, the administrators who in their wisdom did not allow the television to be turned on were giving us frequent updates! We were so aware that many students had parents and family members who worked in the Towers.

As a community, we kept constant vigil on the clock! So we knew that at **9:59 a.m., the South Tower of the World Trade Center began to collapse and as we continued to wait for further development we would learn that** at **10:28: a.m., it was the turn for the North Tower!** The focus of the educators was trained on the students but the thoughts were on the continued developments. As the hours slipped by the original fear that was manifested in the students began to subside, but was quietly increasing in the adults. During that time, the students were engaged in playing games and we began another activity that was our trademark—*Singing*! The calm atmosphere within the storm was only interrupted when a parent appeared to collect a student. At those intervals, we got a bit more information about the outside world that only caused our apprehension to increase.

Lunch came to us compliment of the cafeteria staff. They had pulled all resources together to provide for everyone since we could not return to our rooms. As teachers were given fifteen minutes breaks to talk among ourselves as the news became more and more morbid. Could any more disaster happen in that day? By 2:30 p. m., the last student was picked up and it was the turn of the adults to attempt to find a way home. I began to think... how would I get home? The subways were suspended; the entries and exits between Manhattan, Brooklyn, Staten Island, Bronx, and Queens were blocked. However, we bid each other farewell and began our uncertain journey; we were told that the school's emergency contact tree would be activated and we would know whether there would be school next day.

As I exited the school, the entire atmosphere was filled with the sound of sirens from police vehicles, fire-trucks, and ambulances. The sounds only led to greater anxiety and fear. As I looked at the main street in the Mall, trying to decide which way to turn, I was facing the most amazing and unforget-table sight that has remained with me to this day. I saw an entire line of my fellow humans walking in a daze all covered from head to toe in fine white dust.

In that cloud, there was no distinction between bodies and accessories. No one was speaking just walking as if in a robotic stance.

Slowly, in the greatest state of indecision, I have ever experience, I moved hesitantly towards my usual bus stop, joining the ever-growing groups of confused commuters. Suddenly, a police officer appeared and in a loud voice announced that we should take the bus to the destination... Where was the destination? The driver did not know, but once the bus was filled to capacity, he said he would get some information about the route as we were traveling. The bus flew by all the normal stops and after what appeared to eternity, we were told that this was our destination...

Once I gathered my bearings, I realized that I was still many miles from home. I did not have to remain in this state of confusion for too long because another bus showed up, no fare required. So, we all piled on and were taken to yet another point. After repeating this procedure two more times, it dawned on me that I was inching closer to home! As I would soon realize, the only source of news became word of mouth; <u>technology had lost its power on that day</u>. This was truly a journey, while some left the informal group, others joined, and the conversations became a bit more animated. As individuals joined the group, we got even worse news that **7 World Trade Center, also known as** the Salomon Bros. Building; a 47-story building had sustained damage from falling debris and widespread fires, and had collapsed. What would happen because that building contained New York's emergency operations center?

The most amazing discovery for me was that perfect strangers were actually engaged in conversations with each other. This was not NORMAL, and although I wished it would last; I knew this was an event of short duration. My normal forty or so minute's commute was now four hours but at 7:30 p.m., I was inching closer to home and would be able to walk the final two miles home! Lest I forget, there was one other amazing offshoot of the event—churches overflowed on Sundays; but with time that too gradually changed and in a matter of weeks, it was possible to find a seat in the sanctuary!

As I explained, *Independent School #2* ensured that all members of the community were never alone. Eventually, we received notification, through the television broadcast, that the earliest we would be back in school would be the next Monday. In addition to schools, banks were closed, hospitals were full to overflowing, and the subways did not operate. Although we returned to school the following Monday, September 17th, it would be months before school activities returned to any semblance of normalcy.

The sound of an aircraft flying just too low would produce the immediate response of all eyes looking to the skies. Time is truly able to heal wounds and so it did! However, each anniversary of the disaster—now shortened to 9/11—brought back those stored memories that eat at the soul, the memories, and living! It would be five years later when I decided that if I hoped to maintain my sanity, I would have to leave the city, a place I would always love and will always be HOME! By 2006, I was on to new adventures in another area of the country! I hoped my teaching experiences would continue uninterrupted but elevated!

I continue my contact with so many friends from this school. *Independent School #2* that gave me such a strong foundation as an educator and the institution will always be my HOME. I know that change is a part of life, but I hope the basic principles of the school will be powerful enough to challenge any UNWANTED CHANGES.

So, what made this a great place of learning for all? a) Students were always the first priority; b) peer learning was encouraged so students collaborated to enhance the learning process; c) the educators were qualified professionals who displayed great self esteem; c) Friends' culture fostered an environment where any biases were addressed in community forums between educators, students, and parents—Students had a voice! Parents had a voice! AND the educators and administrators listen to and resolve concerns in order to create a community that was a family of CARING INDIVIDUALS!

Independent School # 3

At the beginning of school year 2006, I was now in a new area of the country and was excited to be teaching in a single-sexed school. As I reflected on my teaching journey, I realized that my first teaching assignment, in Jamaica, was at an all-boys' school for seven years. At that school, I came away with an appreciation of the competitive spirit of my male students. I then followed that journey by teaching at an all–girls' school for four years. Those two assignments allowed me to compare and appreciate the differences in learning styles of the sexes. I am going to generalize here, since the statements will always have exceptions.

As my thoughts traveled over my observations, I realized that male students usually perceive they are super-intelligent even if that is not the case! They generally exude CONFIDENCE! Female students are always asking if they are right as if they never want to be wrong! Male students transfer that air of confidence to every activity compared to female students. In addition, boys need to be constantly moving or doing something (MANUAL DEXTERITY) in order to be stimulated while girls will stay focused, in a sedentary position for long periods. Finally, it would be years later, that I would understand how and why boys process emotional activities in different ways from girls.

As individuals, our learning and thinking are connected to our emotions. As I continue to research those ideas, I recognize that educators create curriculum without demonstrating any clear understanding that boys prefer action while girls prefer interaction. As we educators focus on the learning process of boys and girls, we should become more cognizant of the approaches to ensure that we provide the best opportunities for learning in our future generations. *Well, that would be the subject of another educational chapter or book on learning!*

Sufficed to say, each of those experiences in single-sex schools were new, exciting, and great skill-building opportunities for me as an educator. I was able to understand how to modify those findings when I entered the world of co-ed teaching. I did because I learned very quickly that boys could and would be demanding of the teacher's attention. Therefore, I had to provide opportunities for girls to shine in their own way! I succeeded. Once again, it would take an entire discussion to delve into the techniques that I employed as a science educator during those mixed-group instructional sessions.

The Joy of Teaching and Learning With Great Administrators and Students

So, as I made my adventure into a single-sexed institution for a second time, I wondered how this journey, in a different country and state, would measure up with those prior encounters. I completed an interview in a strange place that was as eye opening as the one I did before entering *Independent School #2*. By the end of the interview session, I knew that once again I had met an individual who cared deeply about educating students. Secretly, I hoped that I would be offered the job because this was the most honest and forthright person.

The Head, Sue T., radiated a love for leading others in their educational pursuits. I did receive the offer and I accepted without hesitation. In time, I would come to respect her honesty and her stance that educators should perform the best job of educating students. She was never afraid to point out, in a supportive way that educators should stay honest, and provide students with the best education.

I also met an Academic Dean who cared deeply about the education of this particular student population. She had clear ideas, and expectations and one could feel her sense of commitment as she engaged in discussions with teachers. I would discover that even if she was at odds with ideas from the teaching staff, she recognized good teaching, and was not afraid to show, and acknowledge those observations in the presence of the community! Within the first few days of the new assignment, I discovered that the students at *Independent School #3* were a joy to teach. They craved new ideas and put effort into learning new concepts. The Head of School, Sue T., recognized the value of providing the best conditions to enhance the learning experiences. Along with the Business Manager, they spared no cost to provide adequate teaching materials to enhance the science program.

Once again, my abilities and skills as a science educator were engaged as I taught Advanced Placement Biology, General Biology, and Environmental Science during my first year. And again, I was able to develop curricular materials appropriate to the age groups, kept the students engaged, excited, and on the path to becoming stewards of the environment. There was no Environment Science curriculum, but there was a textbook! Therefore, I created a syllabus that took my students to places where *FIGMENT* of their imaginations became their close friend. I explained to students that over the years of teaching my animal friend became the Wildebeest (genus *Connochaetes) that inhabits the Serengeti Planes of* Tanzania and Kenya. With that thought, I allowed my students to travel the world to find and learn about exotic plants and animals.

Each student had to become the **FRIEND** of a living organism, and by the end of the mini-unit that culminated in a presentation; students were adept in scientific terminology and applications that included:

1. Taxonomy- Kingdom, Class, Order, Family, Genus, Species.

2. Geological Range.

3. Geographical Range.

4. Ecological Range.

5. Physical Characteristics: Abiotic Factors, Limiting Factors, Biotic Factors including Intra specific relationships - (habitat, niche, home range, female coalitions, male coalitions, communities such as bachelor groups, courting/mating, reproduction) **and** Inter-specific relationships- (biotic pyramids, food chains, herd, predators, parasites, diseases, Man).

6. Adaptations.

7. Zonation and Stratification

8. <u>Ecological Regulations</u>

9. <u>Biogeochemical Cycling.</u>

We created predator-prey games that became the hallmark of our classes. Our travels and discussions gave us an understanding of Gaia[1] and our responsibility to our Earth. I was gratified that several students ventured into studying environmental science and ecology at the tertiary level, and have impacted various countries of our planet such as the Mexico, Haiti, and the Amazon (internships). In all courses, every student was unique and showed such motivation toward learning! I was happy and learning because the students were happy and learning!

Teaching life science to 7th graders was a trip in knowing how to adjust content and skills to meet the needs of the age group. However, I have yet to meet a more motivated group! From the moment that the teaching and learning process began, those students went beyond all expectations. They researched and brought new knowledge to the class for further discussions. They reinforced for me the concept that you can teach anyone any information as long as the knowledge is made applicable to the students' lives.

Those 7th grade students also helped me to learn

---

1   Collins English Dictionary - Complete & Unabridged 10th Edition 2009 © William Collins Sons & Co. Ltd.

more about the complexities of growing up. They would argue with each other one minute, and be the best friends the next minute. Each individual was on a journey to identify one's uniqueness. Many times, emotions spilled over into class discussion, but I did practice—NEVER CORRECT STUDENTS IN FRONT OF THEIR PEERS!! Educators, it is helpful to always separate and diffuse situations… Students will respect you for doing so!

With my 9th graders, we had many adventures on our trips to *Jekyll* and *Tybee Islands* where the environment became our experiential classroom. Students came away as a social unity while learning to appreciate and care for the environment. The students met many of the creatures that we had only seen in our textbook—the loggerhead turtle, the horseshoe crabs, and alligators as we went on night walks, and gathered around the campfires. While those were the best opportunities for learning, the experiences would disappear by the end of the second year! You will learn of the changes in the following pages.

The learning process was just as stimulating as we studied the concepts of Advanced Placement Biology. The course was intense, but as we designed the practical portion that consisted of 12 required labs, our class became more and more animated. We worked together to learn how to use the specialized equipment, ran electrophoresis analysis, bred fruit flies for selected characteristics, and grew to understand the actions of meal bugs. Every day was a fun day even when we had to complete the 20-page lab reports! As a group we would do our frequent walks (one of my peculiarities is that I walk for half-hour each day) to study the plants in the neighborhood. As we walked, we were exercising, and we were learning. **THIS AGAIN WAS TRUE LEARNING**—A credit to the flexibility of learning within an Independent School environment!

In the second year, my assignment was teaching Earth Science to a group of sixth graders in addition to teaching biology to 9th graders, and life science to 7th graders. **I loved the challenge!** Once again, I had only an Earth Science textbook, but I knew how to create curricular material for this age group. We were on a journey through science! We traveled over the tectonic plates of our world, we learned about rocks, and rock formation, made jewelry from the rocks we studied, we learned about hurricanes, tsunami, and traveled (by imagination) to famous volcanoes where our journeys culminated in the *Ancient City of Pompeii*. Three years later, I got a photograph of a geyser from a former sixth grader who had gone to visit the National Parks. I was just as excited when another student explained that the summer trip (2011) involved visits to the workplace of *Maurice Wilkins* and *Rosalind Franklin* (DNA Pioneers), and *Charles Darwin's* grave (Evolution).

The learning and teaching became even more

meaningful as teachers were allowed to take students on learning through taking risks. In the first year, my student became bridge builders as we focused on basic principle of engineering, stitching techniques through needlepoint; and being crime-scene investigators during the microbiology course. I truly believed *Independent School #3* was on the cutting edge of true learning! The conditions were that the institution had the greatest students who wanted to learn. There were educators in all stages of the profession who were willing to find all the means necessary to produce great learning and teaching. However, even if those two sides of the triangle were in place, without a competent and self-assured leadership, the structure is going to be incomplete and subject to failure.

Change (Positive or Negative) Is Inevitable

To my surprise, it would not be long before I would learn the truth behind my observations! Well, the location of the science department required that I had to make an effort to interact with colleagues. Therefore, I was removed from the usual political underpinning of the school community. Day by day, I began to recognize how politics can produce negative changes in a learning environment. *The influence of politics on the operation of independent schools would provide fertile volumes for another book!* Suffice to say, it is amazing to observe how a group or groups with

power, and minimal knowledge of educational principles, could wield influence in terminating administrators and qualified educators.

As I continued my reflection, I believe I was so
focused on adjusting to the new living environment
where I was once again making a 45 minutes commute to work, not with the ease of the New York City
subway, but with high speed traffic that I did not
concern myself with the changes. In this new travel
experience one had to pray that there was no accident on the highway; otherwise, you could be stuck
for hours irrespective of how early you left home.
However, it was my duty to be present on time, so I
made all the effort to be there for my students.

Teaching was my joy! I did not need to adjust. I
was right at home! However, the change in living and
my adjustment must have taken some time because
it took two years to realize that changes were occurring so rapidly around me! By the end of the first
year, the Head of School whom I so respected was on
the way out! The political engine was in full speed!
To this day, I am not aware of the reasons, but the
rumor gave credit to a political force at play. In any
case, there was no one who had any ability to resolve
any of the growing concerns. In time, I would learn
that the culture was one of secrecy, intimidation,
and bullying. I will reflect on my thought regarding
bullying among adults before I close the chapter on

this book. This institution was losing its feeling of *Shangri-La*.

At the beginning of the next school year, the school was now under the guidance of a new interim leader. In addition, several educators were no longer in attendance—they were eliminated quietly. I thought to myself, that in order to move forward, one needed to embrace change. So, I was not distressed because my concern was for the students, and they were as happy and carefree as ever! However, by the end of the second year, the changes could no longer be considered routine!

The interim head was on the way out, the business manager was on the way out, and the Head of Upper School was on the way out. Teaching positions were combined without the least thought about the qualifications and skills of the replacement educators. Soon I would learn that the school did not adhere to any educational philosophy. All actions and thoughts appeared to be based on acquisition of money! Teachers were asked to come up with ways to reduce spending in each department, while the administrators were collecting salaries above $90,000.00. It was as if on a daily basis the school was moving through a dense forest with little regard for the trees! *Could they or were they willing to see the trees?*

The next level of changes came without any warning...the leadership crafted devious ways to eliminate anyone who was either more intelligent, had stronger convictions, or could not be intimidated! I could only anticipate the disaster that those decisions would have on *Independent School #3*.

It became apparent that this school had much to accomplish in educating students, but I wanted to see how the knowledge I had would be used to help in the process. However, disappointment would be the hallmark of my sojourn in the institution. By the start of the third year, there was still no cohesive curriculum. As educators entered the institution, they brought and taught subject matter that they perceived would be important. When those educators left, that information left with them. Even when I was leaving that institution, there was no formal document identifying the skills and knowledge that were the foundation of the school! Would the leaders ever understand that the road to success as an educational institution required leaders who believed in the culture and would be able to develop a unified structure that involved all stakeholders?

What Can Go Wrong Does Go Wrong

My learning really began at the start of my first year. There was a one-week introduction to the instructional design teaching process. That procedure emphasized the teacher as the creator of student learning through the backward design process. At the end of the training, were encouraged to implement the engaging practice in a school-wide effort. Educators were excited, and wanted to implement the new approach but as the year processed and questions about the approach surfaced, there was only one administrator who could answer teachers' questions. Teacher asked for help and direction but they were directed to the text that was provided during the initial workshops or just simply ignored. THIS INSTITUTION TRULY BELIEVED IN THE POWER OF TEXTBOOKS! When teachers could find no support, the initial enthusiasm fizzled. So, the second year arrived with **NO** school-wide curricular document.

I would soon learn that *Independent School #3* exhibited characteristics of a **REACTIONARY** organization with administrators who feared that the incompetence would be uncovered so they could only be described as **RUDE**—*ANOTHER SIGN OF BULLYING AMONG THE ADULT POP-ULATION.* However, I kept my hopes high, and I believed that even if enthusiasm had fizzled, we would revive the most vital component of a school's existence (learning) in the next school year. Well, I was in for major surprise. The backward curriculum design was out—**nothing took its place**—and we were now working on mapping the curriculum for each discipline, **USING THE TEXTBOOKS!** I guess the leaders did not understand that the

only way mapping would work would be to identify links across curricula material. So, we spent the
initial days with **EXPERTS** who were attempting
to teach an entire group to map curriculum when
educators had not identify the content of each curricular area. In addition, the administrators failed
to ask if there were educators within the group
who had prior knowledge of the process. Words of
advice to leaders! **REMEMBER, JUST AS STU-
DENTS LEARN BEST FROM THEIR PEERS...
TEACHERS ALSO LEARN BEST FROM THEIR
PEERS!!!!**

As the process continued, the entire group
of educators, or smaller groups worked on understanding the intricacies of the mapping, but as the
first week ended, teachers had to go back to the real
work—**TEACHING STUDENTS**! As anticipated,
the initial staff meetings and professional development days continued to focus on mapping. However, since some teachers were putting together the
scope and sequence for the subject area content,
only minimal progress was made. In addition, some
of the administrators had no knowledge of mapping techniques; teachers soon became frustrated
and lost their enthusiasm. Suffered to say, the mapping activity never got off the planning stages. That
mapping process became lost in the daily lives of
teachers who were now the instructors, advisors,
attending functions, parent-advisors' meetings,

writing reports, reading reports, and being engaged in other duties that teachers are expected to accomplish at various times throughout the year.

Once again, the discussion of creating a school-wide curriculum reverberated with the arrival of a third school year. By this time, one of the administrators who had any knowledge of curriculum design had left. There was a feeling of despondency even as the first week ended. The new request regarding curricular initiatives was to insert the curricular information taught at the end of each month into a new map. The OLD ONE WAS FORGOTTEN!! After, submission of the skills and concepts, the mapping was checked in the first month, and then the checking just stopped, and the process fizzled. ONCE AGAIN, WE WOULD BE IN THE THIRD YEAR WITHOUT THE SEMBLANCE OF A SCHOOL-WIDE CURRICULUM!

From my observations, there was always excitement with the new learning and upbeat attitude from late August until Thanksgiving. Even if the feelings of goodwill tapered off, as I did observe at other schools, because educators became tired; nothing could be compare to the atmosphere in *Independent School#3*. The sense of uncertainty about jobs began to fill up the rumor-mill from the get go! For fear of losing positions and with the downturn in the economy, cliques developed, people who normally socialized did not even speak with each other! Educators were no longer stopping to speak to each other. Some did not even acknowledge the presence of former friends. This was a toxic bed of mistrust and trepidation! The once lively staff meetings became events where one had to be cautious of every word spoken! As a result, those teachers who continued to participate became ostracized as negative influences or just plain whiners! From my experiences, I knew those words would be used as reasons for dismissal of educators, in the near future.

In addition, the staff meetings became ineffective even with all the new infusion on the part of the administrators who were learning as they go! One of the problems was that the leaders wanted to hear teachers' ideas without explaining what they really wanted. There was this underlying assumption that no one quite understood. Therefore, when the teachers did not comment on the outlandish suggestions that were not related to the welfare of the students, or the instructional process; many found themselves on the outer fringes of the in-group.

Those outsiders were then accused of not helping to move the school in a direction that only administration understood. That was THE PIE IN THE SKY...THE **DIRECTION** WAS NEVER ARTICULATED... It remained in the stratosphere and never came to the ground! TO THIS DAY, THAT STATEMENT CONTINUES TO BE THE REASON

USED BY ADMINISTRATORS TO RELIEVE TEACHERS OF THEIR POSITIONS!

The New Dismissal Process

That was just one reason among the other inventive reasons I did hear. Sometimes the grounds for teacher dismissal were far more devious. One such case came when one educator was informed, two years after she left, that the reason for asking her to leave was that she did not continue to associate with a specific group—the **IN-GROUP**, but instead had become friends with a <u>black </u>educator! As I continued to reflect, I came to discover the racist underpinnings of the institution. However, far be it from the administrators who professed that the institution was an all-inclusive organization that displayed no biases! **ALL ARE WELCOME!!!** *The leaders of Independent School #3* had it all wrong—No school can survive where COVERT RACISIM CONTINUES TO REAR IT UGLY HEAD! Due diligence is a must if any parent would consider enrolling a child in such a place of learning.

Although I believed I had seen and experienced all that could go wrong at any independent school; I was in for a GREAT SURPRISE! In 2009, several staff members were released from this independent school for frivolous reasons, not suggested openly, but the rumor-mill came up with the following:

1. You were perceived to be too negative; or

2. You did not hang out with your colleagues–staff who used to visit at the "water-cooler", and speak negatively about other staff members, parents, and administrators; or

3. You had too much knowledge that you failed to share with administration so they could assimilate your ideas as their own; and

4. You associated with people who were not of your own race!

The administration never verbalized those comments instead the reason given to all was that the student enrollment had declined. As it would turn out, the next school year would see a rise in enrollment! To top this all, educators were threatened by the unscrupulous administrators of the consequences for discussing their dismissal with anyone! The **ACT OF BULLYING, WHO SAYS IT ONLY EXISTS AMOMG THE STUDENT POPULATION?** Still, I continue to question how this can be happening in a country such as ours where DEMOCRACY is ours RALLY CRY! *How can it be that educators who have invested so much time, energy, and finances have no recourse within our system?*

The Leaders Who Cannot Lead

This was my first experience with individuals who were given position without the basic qualification and who either did not have MORAL COMPASSES or had lost their MORAL COMPASSES along the way. No school can exist or survive without knowledgeable, intelligent, or moral leaders. Unfortunately, the leaders of *Independent School #3* allowed the institution to suffer from persistent identity crisis! The leaders were egotistical, glory-seeking bullies who had little or no interest in the population of learners that they served. The lack of knowledge and skills in administration will forever keep those leaders in a state of **MENTAL SLAVERY**!

I did not realize that others were internalizing the problem until I read the thoughts of one educator who laid out the view that many outstanding educators lost their teaching positions because the school was more interested in saving money rather than providing quality education for the students. That life-changing experience was the perfect example that what can go wrong does go wrong! A culture developed within that institution where **NO ONE TRUSTED ANYONE**! So many lives were damaged in the process, but I can see that those educators who were affected rose up and continue to stand tall, much taller than those who tried to do such wrongs!

Change! Change! Change

Our country cannot afford to have institutions, such as *INDEPENDENT SCHOOL #3* that continues to exist without some form of proper supervision and guidance. Those issues outlined above must not be hidden, but must be documented so we can better understand where the problems lie as we try to educate our next generation. While there are schools that are in the business of educating our students in the best way, there are others such as *INDEPENDENT SCHOOL #3* that require focused monitoring. Although, such institutions are private entities, there must be a process of accounting to ensure that such schools are doing what they say they do, and putting them out of business if they do not meet with stringent guidelines. *My question is who will step forward to unearth those guiding principles and when will such strategies be established or enforced?*

Therefore as educators in this great nation, the question becomes who will develop or enforce the oversight processes that might need to be awakened? I would talk directly to the members of the accreditation agencies and encourage the visiting educators to recognize that information provided during the accreditation visits is most often accurate, but in some cases might be sugar-coated and glazed over. The question is–how does the agency get to the truth? **DELVE DEEPER!** I am speaking from experience as a veteran educator that there is no way to visit every four or five years, then make site observations and be able to recognize the problem. There is just too much turnover of personnel during the interim. There must be a way to acquire and analyze attrition and retention data and so determine the need for interim visits. The accreditation team has to investigate the problems—believe me they exist... then those problems MUST BE evaluated.

I proposed that such action might address the issues facing institutions such as *INDEPENDENCE SCHOOL #3*. Further, it is important that the accrediting agency listens carefully to the answers to questions about the school's operations and life. I have heard the *telltale signs* in people's words, and recognize the responses through their body language. The glazing over of the system before and during the accreditation process must be **seen for what is. Additionally, I propose that such institutions implement exit interviews of administrators, faculty, and staff and that the findings be incorporated into future evaluations by the accreditation teams**.

Once those details are reviewed then organizations such as *Independent School #3* would be required to address the issues. Thus, many present and potential problematic situations might be resolved. At *Independent School #3*, the last qualified administrator with any experience or training left in 2011. *Change must occur!* How can an educator deliver consequences to students for plagiarism when the educator, is doing the same? How can an educator just use TESTS and GRADED DISCUSSIONS as the method of grading students so that the majority of the class receives grades of A? Can we, as educators, blame students when they fail to succeed at the tertiary level because they lack basic knowledge and skills?

My Suggestions to Future Parents and Guardians

Present and future parents must begin to ask tough questions of schools such as ***INDEPENDENT SCHOOL #3.***

- Can you outline the educational philosophy on which your school operates?

- What are the qualifications of the educators? Are they certified? Does having a master in philosophy provide an educator with the understanding of who should be employed to guide students?

- How would you explain the high level of attrition in educators?

- How do you explain the number of leaders who have left the school within the last ten years?

- Who is responsible for evaluating potential

educators, and do those individuals have expertise in evaluating resumes? That is important since no professional would respond to a candidate's resume with the statement that the candidate's resume would be **KEPT IN THE HEAP**!

At *Independent School #3*, there has been a full turnover of educators within two years, and now three years later, as I reviewed the new additions to the team; it is apparent that the administration has not increased in wisdom! Of the fourteen and potentially more new additions, very few have any experience in the roles that they will assume. It is my fervent belief that over time, educators do learn if they are given the opportunity and training. However, students do not have the luxury of waiting for people to learn in order to teach or guide them.

The culture of dishonesty continues and I will wait to see the repeat turnover at the end of year three. I have come to the conclusion that this is a perfect example of an institution where the head wants to establish a name! How else could one explain the departure of **every** administrator within one school year? Where is the tradition or foundation that will be used to support the infrastructure of that school?

Let us work to fix such institutions because a house divided against itself will fall.

Closing Thoughts

As an educator, the transition to independent school environment is not without issues. It requires a shift in thinking and mindset for any educator, and coupled with the increased political atmosphere, many instructors find survival to be fleeting!

In addition, while I applaud the investigations and actions on BULLYING among the student populations; what about the **BULLING PRACTICES AMONG THE SCHOOL'S ADULT POPULATION? This area must be investigated to ensure survival of gifted educators in this country's educational systems.**

As the consummate science educator, I know all children are brim full of curiosity and motivation! So why do we allow the creativity and enthusiasm to die? Each individual is a unique creation, and our goal as educators is to become adept at allowing the gifts of all children to shine through. We can no longer be satisfied that the creation and procreation of one curriculum will fit the needs of all children!

The road to reform is achievable; we have no shortage of creative and skill minds in our population of educators!

Would someone help me to identify those educated, creative minds who cannot find employment, so we can once again put a system in place that will allow this great country to

return to its Number 1 position as an educational leader?

CPSIA information can be obtained at www.ICGtesting.com
Printed in the USA
LVOW05s1514141213

365169LV00001B/1/P